Other Books by John Bradley

POETRY
Dear Morpheus, The Glue That Is You (2023)
Hotel Montparnasse: Letters to César Vallejo (2021)
Everything in Motion, Everything at Rest (2020)
Spontaneous Mummification (2020)
Agitprop (2019)
Erotica Atomica (2017)
And Thereby Everything (2015)
Love-In-Idleness: The Poetry of Roberto Zingarello (2015)
One Day You a Mountain Shall Be: The Lost Poetry of Cheng Hui (2014)
You Don't Know What You Don't Know (2010)
Terrestrial Music (2006)
Add Musk Here (2002)
To Dance with Uranium (1995)
The New Wine Dreaming in the Vat (1993)
From the Faraway Nearby (1992)
Love-In-Idleness: The Poetry of Roberto Zingarello (1989)
All for Blanca (1988)
A-E-I-O-U (1981)

PROSE
Trancelumination (2011)
War on Words (2006)

ANTHOLOGIES
And Blue Will Rise Over Yellow: An International Poetry Anthology for Ukraine (2023)
Eating the Pure Light: Homage to Thomas McGrath (2009)
Learning to Glow: A Nuclear Reader (2000)
Atomic Ghost: Poets Respond to the Nuclear Age (1995)

AS BLOOD
IS THE FRUIT OF
THE HEART

A Book of Spells

JOHN BRADLEY

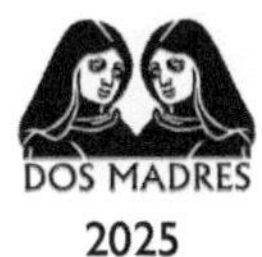

DOS MADRES

2025

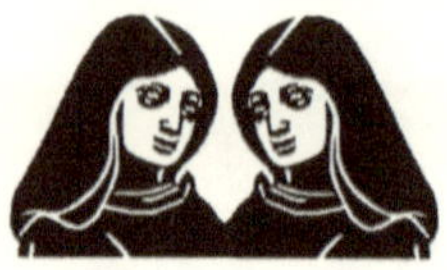

DOS MADRES PRESS INC.
P.O. Box 294, Loveland, Ohio 45140
www.dosmadres.com   editor@dosmadres.com

Dos Madres is dedicated to the belief that the small press is essential to the vitality of contemporary literature as a carrier of the new voice, as well as the older, sometimes forgotten voices of the past. And in an ever more virtual world, to the creation of fine books pleasing to the eye and hand.

Dos Madres is named in honor of Vera Murphy and Libbie Hughes, the "Dos Madres" whose contributions have made this press possible.

Dos Madres Press, Inc. is an Ohio Not For Profit Corporation and a 501 (c) (3) qualified public charity. Contributions are tax deductible.

Executive Editor: Robert J. Murphy

Illustration & Book Design: Elizabeth H. Murphy
www.illusionstudios.net

Typeset in Adobe Garamond Pro & Snell Roundhand
ISBN 978-1-962847-18-6
Library of Congress Control Number: 2024952674

GRATITUDE

I am indebted to Remedios Varo, whose "A Recipe: How to Produce Erotic Dreams" sparked this book of spells. I am also grateful for the kindness of friends: Ric and Bonnie Amesquita, Marilyn and Cliff Cleland, Joe and Jean Gastiger, George Kalamaras, Ken Letko, Becky Parfitt, Susan and Christopher Porterfield.

For Jana

Table of Contents

BOOK FIVE

BOOK SIX

I put a spell on you.

—Screamin' Jay Hawkins

*The origins of poetry are clearly rooted in obscurity,
in secretiveness, in incantation,
in spells that must at once invoke and protect,
tell the secret and keep it.*

—Mary Ruefle

PREMONITION THAT A BOOK WILL TAKE THE SHAPE
OF A SPELLBOUND BIRD

When a spell enters the mouth, three strands of sea-green
silk go flying over the ocean. It could be noted they smell

like a pickle left on a plate before a blindfolded surgeon.

Thrumming and humming, the silk strands melt above
the White Sands Desert. When a spell enters the mouth,

at the edge of the cosmos, I know I'll never need

another paper cello lit from within. Though one day
a postage stamp will choke a hummingbird and no one

will be there to witness the fish bowl where a heart

with fins and gills swims in circles. When a spell enters
the mouth, that red metal toolbox you found in the cornfield

won't unlock. Because a spell can't be tricked, rubbed,

licked, robbed, kissed, caged, killed, swallowed. Because
in the oven, it never rains, even when it rains. Because

upstairs, even now, Adolf Eichmann feeds a sugar cookie

to his pet rat. But the storied tongue: It flits, flutters, forgets
everything it's told us. Even as the spell—as if foretold—

through the body unfolds.

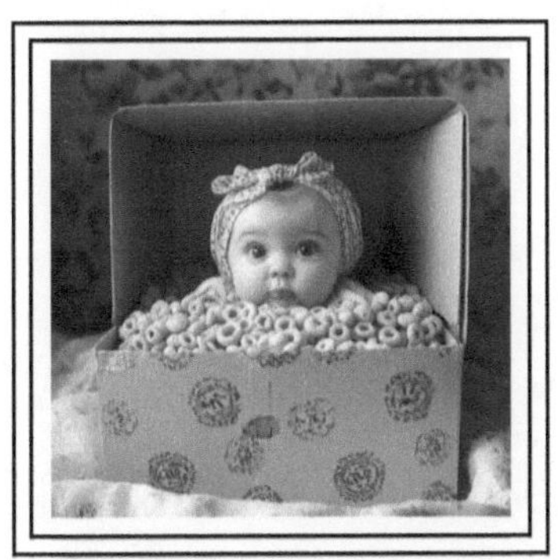

BOOK ONE

Five Definitions of *Spell*

Close your eyes and find yourself asleep somewhere
inside a hazy tree. Tell me your flesh isn't
the color of the nearest sky.

*

You don't like my hat of febrile star matter. I don't
much like your pulsating, chrome green Van Gogh
glow-in-the-dark money clip.

*

You can subdivide a rat into nine crows, each
clutching a ravenous pencil, though the nine birds
and the nine pencils will not be able to draw
a functioning rat.

*

I remember when you were a sapling with long
blonde hair wavering before a door to a place
that exists only when you read this spell aloud.

*

In any vein, bits of cricket song and the yearning
of vernal trees dappled with babbling birds.

Spider Spell(s)

1.
Spiders speak 1,926 languages.
I have many holes in my memory I can't blame on a spider.
You won't be waving your tongue at me like that after
          the spider bite.

Those rounded croutons in your green pea soup—spider eggs.
You were going on and on about how spider silk is stronger
          than steel, tougher than Kevlar—and the cat yawned.
Genevieve wouldn't talk to me after I ran over her spider
          in the driveway.

Where's D. B. Cooper? Down the basement, sleeping
          with the spiders.
You spider-walked across the living room ceiling and Jesus
          Christ was loudly summoned a goodly number
          of times.
Your mother screamed when your hand was briefly a black
          widow spider.

Remember, a spider can be reassembled hundreds of times.
Don't tell me that wasn't you writhing around in a web last
          night.
Remedios Varo had a recipe for healing a crack in the ceiling
          calling for fresh spider eggs.

I have absolutely nothing against meteors, plagues, spiders,
          and celebrity poetry.
Saliva is not the cure, said the spider, *for the cure is not saliva.*
My all-too-quiet, all-too-smart neighbor, the spider.

2.
At the center of each web, notes *Remain Calm:*
The Window Washer's Portable Handbook,
a sticky spell of silence.

3.
The wind keeps blowing whatever it keeps blowing
        from the Spider Zone.
My first wife was the third cousin of a woman often called
        the Embodiment of the Fiftieth Spider.
In Oklahoma, they call spiders Bombay blossoms.

But how long can you hold your tongue on an ice cube
        with a spider resting in your voice box?
In sixth grade, I sat on a spider in science class; no one
        applauded.
When Ambassador Spider enters the room, do not blink.

OK, I've never danced naked with a spider, but I once
        did wrap a wounded tongue with a spider web.
Listen to them, the spirits in the wall, breathe spider psalm.
I read to the assembly a list of all the curses directed
        at spiders; it went on for six hours.

Don't make a move, says my life coach, *when spider-bidden.*
The spider-tamer has never gotten on with the spider-rider.
Where's Amelia Earhart? In the attic, reading Emily
        Dickinson to the spider mother superior, her eight
        eyes shifting back and forth.

Jimmy Hoffa? Still following the endless spider thread
        he swears will lead him back to the Red Fox
        Restaurant.
The Representative from the Nonaligned Spiders International
        Chapter is waiting for you now under the sink.
Doctor on a donkey, nurse in a hearse, spider in the revolver
        in the baby carriage.

4.
You live deep inside a spinneret, friend,
and no one will tell you
but me.

PLACENTAL GRAVITY SPELL

I was born in a box of Cheerios, inside the pantry, near the
        broom and the bison.
I was born in my mother's armpit, her stubbly flesh smelling
        of a pickle barrel.
I was born behind a common comma, mapping out
        the whirling world of my coma.
I was breathing through the pores in my feet, pouring out
        a fog which would later say, *Edgar Allen Poe poured*
        whiskey on his Wheaties.
I was born with my head in my mouth, tongue in my brain,
        my blood pounding this refrain: *Each song leaves you*
        with a clutch of sugar, a clutch salt.
I closed my eyes, stars burning through my eyelids, so many
        stars I knew they had to be rhythm and riddle.
I closed my eyes, and I could see Walt Whitman humping
        a support beam on the Brooklyn Bridge, Herman
        Melville in the planetarium huffing whale blubber,
        Emily Dickinson in a black veil scrawling her birth
        name on the belly of a tomato worm.
I was breathing through every line and stanza I had yet
        to write, words floating just above and below the colon
        in my heart, telling me: *Unbind yourself from the hands*
        of the clock, even as the numbers blister, as they snap, crackle,
        pop.
I was breathing in all the cigarette smoke I would ever choke
        on, mulching it into dead leaves.
My first words were *Hello, Placental Gravity. Hello, Slug*
        in the Coffee Can Soaking in Kerosene.
My first words were *Everyone, take to your bomb shelter now. Leave*

behind your welts and shredded wheat.
I was, I were, and yet I was not yet fully born. This all
      happened when it will happen, only then and now.
No, I was born on the back of a velvet ant, wearing a tin
      crown. Laden with Lucky Charms.

In Coral Gables, Florida, today, a man invented a new word
        for *nonflammable knee.*
In Toledo, Ohio, a woman boiled a pot of green pea soup
        into a headache.
In San Diego, California, a retiree was found living in the back
        of the mouth of a former physicist.

In Poland, New York, a child located the Warsaw Ghetto
        in a sewer drain pipe.
In Port Townsend, Washington, a parrot said to its owner, *You
        may call me Thorazine, but don't try to call me Thor.*
In Galveston, Texas, small, jagged pieces of Maine were found
        in a ravine.

In Valley Stream, Long Island, a tongue escaped the mouth
        of a dog and was eventually found stuck to the side
        of a beehive.
In Bayfield, Wisconsin, a resident heard Lake Superior
        murmur, *My brain is almost transparent.*
In South Bend, Indiana, a loaf of rye bread settled at the top
        of a poplar. It had flown from a Panera in Portland.

In Wheeling, West Virginia, a crowd of crows dove into
        an open thermos of rattled coffee. They have yet to emerge.
In Death Valley, California, a bird made of human and animal
        teeth was observed trying to eat a boulder.
In Cairo, Illinois, a piece of Asheville was found in a bowl
        of Froot Loops. No word yet of any dental injury.

In Moab, Utah, Thursday night invaded a home, sealed
        the windows and doors, and devoured all available
        electrical power.
In Pocatello, Idaho, a hair dryer was found plugged into
        a potato. It's been said to be running for at least
        twenty-nine days.
In Washington, D.C., a cracked cinder block was seen mating
        with the White House.

In Bloomington, Minnesota, a snowman entered the Mall
        of America and urinated on a small dog.
In Truth or Consequences, New Mexico, an opera singer
        opened her mouth in her driveway. An X in the shape
        of an X emerged.
In Coral Gables, Florida, the new word for *nonflammable knee*
        was just named the state bird song.

(FURTHER EVIDENCE OF A)
   SPONTANEOUS MUMMIFICATION SPELL

The woman who plays harmonica with a tarantula in her
          mouth, who will tell you, each time you ask, *The human
          tongue has far too many bones.*

The ants eating a white plastic fork, without ever asking
          the white plastic fork, *What color is the black Tin Lizzie
          Henry Ford was buried in?*

The NSA contractor, who falls asleep at 3:43:02 a.m., who
          wakes at 3:43:29 to find the steel door to the Operation
          Center a throbbing artichoke.

The judge who uses a sock puppet to instruct the jury, the jury
          that replies by rapidly blinking their eyes.

The Secretary of Aliens Amongst Us, who will eat not
          of terrestrial flesh, but only of fibrous growth, nibbles
          on his silk suit the color of mummified sky.

The Professor of the Literature of Opioid Addiction who tells
          the class, *Paint a picture of Wrigley Field as an intergalactic
          vehicle on the last day.*

The pancake in the IHOP that sprouts eyes, which track
          the toads gathering on the ceiling, which gaze upon
          the upside-down glass of water near the pancaked plate.

The electronic device at the meeting that sometimes asks to be
        called *I-am-your-good-friend Bob*, and other times *How-can-
        anyone-not-like-a-tube-sock.*

The cactus juggler, and part-time avian linguist, who stops
        to eat a cotton ball whenever an airborne cactus says,
        It takes a sutured eye to see the sutured moon.

The buff hen, without a visible head, who wanders the hallway
        murmuring, *I am that which knoweth not ought nor nought.*

The president who looks into his presidential mouth mirror
        and spies on his blistered tongue a portrait
        of the president, with a portrait of the president
        on his blistered tongue.

The buff hen, still without a head, who murmurs, *Whereupon
        thy left hand shall mightily smite thee, even as thy righteous brain
        proclaims: This too is true.*

Spell for a Photo of the Moon at the Moment of My Birth

I am six years old. I don't know who put this open cigar box
on my head. Maybe it was me.

I'm eighteen. At the mouth of the driveway, I'm taking
a photo of the moon with a broken camera. The moon is
naked and nervous and flirty.

I am nine years old. I'm keeping a diary called *The Rain Is Not
My Father.* My father burns it.

I'm a year and a half, lying inside a wooden cage. There's
an entity in the hallway quietly saying my name over and
over. I pretend I can't hear it.

I am five years old. A big dog with a huge mouth chases me
around a car. I climb up on the hood and tell the hairy
beast: *Jesus fire come down on you.*

I am ten. The face under the cowboy hat is so blurred
I'm not sure this boy is really me. The black cowboy boots
pinch my toes.

I'm thirteen. I've just taken my father's Colt .45 from under
his mattress and buried it in the backyard sandbox. He doesn't
yet know what I've done. I don't yet know what he'll do.

I am zero years old, napping in this pulsing pillow where I pay
no rent. My mother says I've squatted here for ten long
months. She wants me evicted—now. The moon, as anyone
can see, is full.

SPELL FOR THE PERSISTENCE OF DESIRE

And then and then and then and then.
–Pablo Neruda, tr. Alastair Reid

I remember that drugstore in Duluth where I called
the police to ask if they knew the capital of Minneapolis.

I can remember watching Andy Warhol filming
a wedding in West Duluth, though he made me promise to tell
no one he had a cousin who lived there.

I remember that brick house in Lynbrook where
everyone who entered fell asleep. They had to be carried out
on stretchers. *That's what happens to anarchists*, my mother
said.

I remember shoveling sand into burlap sacks the day
Kennedy was shot, stacking them along the base of our house
with my father, sister, mother, brother.

I remember the day I found the white-uniformed
milkman passed out beneath the pear tree in our backyard,
at his side, a half-empty bottle of chocolate milk.

I remember my Irish grandmother from Brooklyn
scratching as she cried, crying as she scratched a hole near
her ankle, swearing, then apologizing to God.

I remember getting seasick on the Cyclone at Coney
Island, but I don't believe those who say I fainted and flew out
of the car.

I remember the gravel driveway where I floated above
the heads of the kids who couldn't see me, and above
the heads of those who could.

I still remember the shark in the back of the pickup
truck at Key West, flies praising the persistence of desire.
I remember buying shots of rum for the deputy and
the reporter and chasing the Cuban who bit my ear.

I remember that Saturday in Minneapolis when two
women in heels stood at the door. They wanted to know if
I had sinned, if I could imagine the end of the world, and what
would I do for the children of Peru. Why the dark-haired one,
Michaela, agreed to marry me, I still don't know.

But mostly, I remember crossing the field
to the airstrip in Germany. I squeezed my father's hand, wild
onions sprouting from his chest. I could hear him calling me,
but no sound would leave my throat. I watched as he dug
a hole in the field and poured gasoline over my clothes.
The onions swaying side to side in the breeze.

Spell for a Tumultuous Tongue

Look at this strange creature, beached so far
from its home. What made it roam?

Was it in search of food? Desiring a mate?

Was it exhausted by the journey and no longer
can stir? Or perhaps it's deceased? Wait,

it's swaying side to side, stretching, rubbing,

worming about. All the while, firmly rooted
to the floor. Surely it must tire of being

permanently tethered. How odd it possesses

no tusk, horn, claw, or tooth. It can't sting
or bite to defend itself. Even if you poked

this featureless beast with a sharp stick.

Nevertheless, I find myself a bit uneasy
around the tongue, as if at any second

it could suddenly lash out. But this is

nonsense. Allow the tongue to rouse
and meekly lick your outstretched hand.

SPELL FOR THE CURRENT STATE OF FERAL RAPTURE

There was a bowl of smoke, hazy blueish smoke, lingering
in the bowl before him, saying, *Long ago I was once
a semisolid, like you.*

*

You no doubt record me each night in the bathroom, his
complaint states, *as I wash my words, long before they leave
my mouth.*

*

The farther down the spiral stairs to the center of the Earth
he went, the louder the pounding of the language forge.

*

He left me his personal copy of that six-hundred-and-one
page governmental report on *The Current State of Feral
Rapture*, his spidery red ink in the margin, declaring, *Kettle
drums! Glockenspiel!*

*

On the arrest warrant, it states that he sawed a cello in half
with malice aforethought, but he claims he was hired to do
so by the owner, who swore a boa constrictor lived inside
his beloved cello.

*

Each time I blink, I age another year in a universe not that distant from the one you and I presently reside in, he told the census worker.

*

Facing the firing squad, his tongue kept twisting, trying to pry out that raspberry seed stuck between his two back teeth. *Just another minute,* he said, *and I'll be ready.*

SPELL FOR A PIECE OF MT. EVEREST
    GLOWING IN A SUITCASE

In my hair is all history, all / bloodred atlases.
–Tomaž Šalamun, tr. Brian Harvey

Dear Tomaž, should I pack my cranky winter socks?
Will you bring your polar-ice-powered TV?

Remind me, how did we say we'll dismantle Mt. Everest?
Brick by brick? Drop by drop? Why is it so much easier

to speak to you through a toothbrush? Even as you slip
across the border into amnesia. Right now tiny sparks

in your brain keep whirring along the electric fence
surrounding Amazonia. Creatures like you diving

into and out of creatures like me. Don't worry, my false
passport will scare off the the fear of a flying fox.

Have you ever yelled at a doctor in French as you fell
through the spaces between his teeth? Whiskey can wake

a dead horse for nine seconds. The danger—one human-
to-animal breath can ignite a moon. All night I wondered:

Is a bucket of memory oil the same as a bucket of otter
drift? It's true, images of sleepers inhaling sleep can be

a bit erotic.   As if you were eating turtle soup out of a papier
mâché turtle. Just as we leave, Tomaž, tell me again:

Sometimes be afraid of the sometimes-human voice.

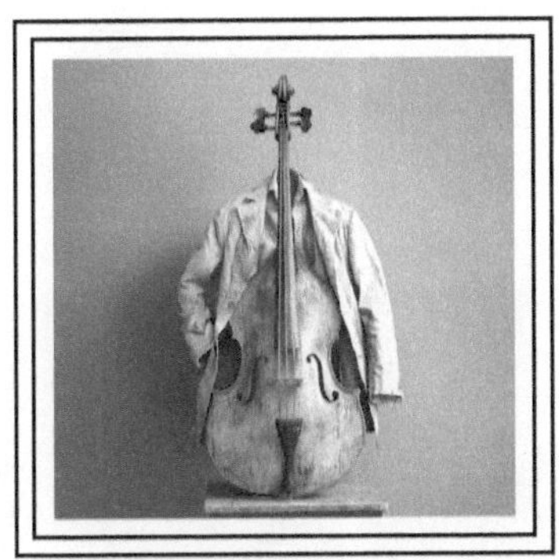

BOOK TWO

FIVE DEFINITIONS OF *SPELL*

Right after she was singed by the saucepan, Ophelia
covered the dining room walls with a sticky,
venomous vine.

*

I don't see through clothing; I simply see old musical
instruments wearing your pants and shirt and coat.

*

All those disembodied leaves—an angel with a bejeweled
cigarette lighter called them *aimless, shambling, featureless
oracles.*

*

A few hours later, we were cheered to hear a $100 baked
potato survived a fall from a tall building. Unlike the polar
bear with the velvet violet umbrella.

*

Dear Tao Yuanming, the body is an egg filled with
students who say, *I draw what I see, and all I see is the inside
of a creature that long ago shed its wings.*

Because Everyone Loves a Love Spell,
    However, Whosoever

The psychopharmacologist mannequin is shoeless.
The Amazon is sick from reading too much Oscar Michaux.

When I was a high school student mannequin, the Algebra

teacher mannequin got hives and disappeared into respiratory
needs. Thou shalt not nudge or budge the weightless hand.

Tell me, love, about that spiral spiraling in your gut. Do not

buy a crocodile or a clock dial from a wheelwright in Ireland.
Digesting a metal atom divides intervals into serrated breath.

A gun can be folded into a box of Wheaties, into any

prepositional phrase. For the spiral, you once told me, will
outlive Ashbery and Bolaño. Soon we will meet in 1938,

at a Nazi youth camp on Long Island. Thou shalt not

nudge or budge the weightless hand. Which means:
Moroccan bread, seam stress, cognac, adverb, multiple-choice

cancer, poem that doubles as handy household hacksaw.

How to Have Sex in a Canoe

To avoid capsizing, use bold geometric patterns. Freud
described carnal pleasure as *the classification of the terrifying
which leads back to the center of gravity.* Take some basic
vowel precautions—turn to Machu Picchu, the Acropolis,

Pompeii. In the event of a flip, the aura is sucked clean out.
Beginners should try a glassy-eyed mannequin dressed in neon
dreams. You may decide to remove your life jacket
or linger without a partner. Freud says, *Suspended animation*

remains a perverse satisfaction. Be mindful of black fly
YouTube videos. Orgasmic rivers and streams on an altered
plane. Anne Sexton, hugging her effigy. You don't want
to get stuck in a shipwreck in Iowa at 18. Somebody

who knows corporeal satisfaction might wish for a living,
breathing person. Don't forget the Milky Way, perched
on a trumpet, waiting for your hips to roll with the canoe.
Visceral magnetism. Effigies torn apart. You can see

Whitman's chamber pot, Machu Picchu, Pompeii,
the Acropolis. You can see Sylvia Plath in an apple tree
in Frederick, Md. Suspended levitation a terrifying
pleasure. Resist your own erasure. Balance the cosmos.

How to Protect Yourself from a Love Spell

On a purple afternoon looted from a monastery in 1917,
wear an aspirin behind each eye. Say to the hotel manager

in Greenland, *I need to protect my raving vocabulary from your roving
headache.* Find four carriers of salt, whether a small baggie

of salt crumbs, or a forty-pound bag of lunar salt. Tell
the chef, *But I don't participate in a clear narrative.* Dream

you find a small tattoo of an ear inside your right ear. Fold
here. Cut here. Waver here. Say, when no one is around,

I'm almost sea ice now, and *Irradiated faces see irritated vases.* Beware
any mention of sleep incantation. Beware wavy lines, porous

and ripe. Keep the four carriers of salt at all times at an equal
distance around your body, whether arranged about you

in a square or diamond. Avoid hearing the manicurist tell
you, *Because beetles are something people step on.* The raving.

The roving. Keep the carriers of salt from licking any tree
with charred bark wrapped in tin foil. Above all, avoid

the translator of whale song into elephant tusk, who will
tell you, behind each eye, *I see traces of sleep excavation.*

Spell for the *Barbenheimer* Mutations

In Barbie's white, cat-eyed sunglasses—roiling, rolling atomic fire.

*

Her bodacious blond hair gushing up into a mushroom cloud,
Barbie confesses: *This Ken is a stylist.*

*

A cuddly Ken crows: *I am become Ken, Destroyer of Beach.*

*

In their sleek, pink convertible, Barbie and Ken cruise
the desert, a perfectly pink mushroom cloud blossoming
behind them.

*

Cowgirl Barbie in pink jumpsuit shakes hands with J. Robert
Oppenheimer, his civilian-military-scientist-professorial suit
aflame.

*

Sporting a knowing smile, Oppie glows, a massive mushroom
cloud ascending a mountain range behind him, while
an offscreen Barbie coos: *Come on, Bobby, let's go party.*

*

A hunky Oppenheimer with a long-legged Barbie perched
on his shoulder, the firestorm raging behind them not daring
to ignite the oh-so-polite palm trees.

*

Two torn half-faces fitted together: In Barbie's sunglass lens,
Trinity simmers; in J. Robert's lens, a slinky-pink highway
unwinds.

*

Take the bathroom tissue test: Pink or black? *Are you Barbie or
Oppenheimer toilet paper?*

*

Half black-hatted, half-white hatted, this two-faced creature
states: *I am become Barbie, Destroyer of Worlds.*

*

Blindingly blonde Barbie, wildly waving her white hat while
astride that nasty, naughty infernal gadget.

*

O look and see what Little Boy did to Barbie Land. All
the dreamy Dreamhouses—Hiroshimaed. Chorus the Kens
and Barbies: *The horror! The horror!*

Spell for the Fluttering in Your Right Leg

Visit, at the bird sanctuary, three mouthless angels
bearing coffee-maker wounds. Interview anyone
connected with the sale of *glandular wisdom of the ages*.

Do not mention the rise of Nazi animal anatomy
without harp, celesta, and woodwinds. Rendered invisible,
Buenos Aires dawdles in your synthetic basement.

Visit your private cumulus cloud traversing above
France as a hand-rolled cigarette. The surface
of your tongue against the surface of my heart,

with countless little murmurs. On the fourth floor,
announce: *Aviator towels, paintbrush tyrant, heavy
rubato, lemon-lime violin.* Spend at least ten minutes

on the ladder siphoning ambient electricity into
your spine. Speak Spectral-English to Carl Jung's
owl scalpel, ninety seconds away from flickering

birds. Praise the chips of glacial ice, but do not
call them *gastral light.* Steal from the hand that holds
Dostoyevsky's bag of sharpened teeth. Buenos Aires

dawdling in your basement. Repeat at intervals
of twenty-one seconds: *After the human body cools—
a thousand fluted light bulbs lit by drifts of random*

solitude. Admit you see a square triangle secreting
a triangular square. The surface of your tongue against
the surface of my heart, with countless little murmurs.

SHOULD A BLUE SHIRT YOUR WAY COME FLYING SPELL

Should a blue shirt come flying, flying over the water

check your pocket for faux lint, faux forest, faux
woodwind, faux midnight with faux black hair.

Pay close attention to the edge of page that's crumbling.

What can you say to the wandering wheatfield?
I'm sorry for the sorry ants. Who are never sorry.

The blue shirt, over the water, it keeps flying, flying.

Yes, I have eaten of this silence and the silence
has eaten of me. This is the sound that convulsed

Sylvia Plath one night in a laundromat in Paris.

But a mouse in a lightbulb is not the same as
a lightbulb inside a mouse. Over the water, the blue

shirt flying, flying still. This is the last thing

the moment needs to say. Pay close attention
to the molecular matter of the tongue, now transparent,

now not. Any goldfish on the moon will tell you.

TWENTY QUESTIONS FOR THE MOON
(NOT THAT IT NEEDS A SPELL)

How is it I can fit the Nile River in an eyedropper
but not your delicious light? Spilling, plunging,
surging—which best describes the hunger of your
Sea of Fecundity? If I make a crooked circle
with forefinger and thumb, hold it up until it
surrounds you, will you blind me, or make me
surrender to wakeful sleep? On that plaza in Manaus
named for you? What was it Li Po said
when he sank into your long cadaverous arms?
Tell us, why is NASA hiding our kidnapped children
in colonies on Mars? Plunging, surging, spilling—
which best describes your vaporous white hair?
On that steep street in Galway named for you?
When Galileo gazed through his telescope
at your granulated flesh, how softly did he say,
I am made of moon and ravenous rib and waterless river?
Do you prefer being compared to a peeled lemon,
slice of unripe banana, or hammered tin head?
On that back street in Reykjavik named for you?
Is it true you keep a list of every fool
who ever mooned you? Surging, spilling, plunging—
how is it you shadow me by day, I shadow you
by night? O carnivorous moon, may I serve you
at the Banquet of Luminous Beings? On plates
of damp moonstone? With narcotic blooms
of moonflower? In Novosibirsk, near
the unfinished nuclear waste repository,
in the middle of the roundabout named for you?

What was it you told Li Po when he embraced
your surging, spilling, plunging arms? When
will we build a delirious wall to keep you
from seeping into our dream reservoir? Why
did you tell those moonstruck kids NASA kidnapped
and sent to Mars, *If you wear silver gloves
no one will be able to withstand
the beauty of your vaporous hands?*

Shakespeare, They Say, Did Not Always Spell His Own Name the Same Way

He carved each letter into the page, his vowel-swallowing,
trance-inducing name, but when done he found his pen had
scrawled: *Somnambulantblur*.

*

He stared, glared at the letters, fuzzy blackish-blue and blueish-
black, and watched them meander about the page, some
scratching themselves, others flying off across the room
to buzz against the window.

*

He focused first on the word *Shake* and his hand would shake.
He focused even harder on the word *Spear* and his quill struck
the paper like a spear piercing the side of a boar.

*

Maybe if he wrote the last letter first and the first letter last,
the task of getting all the letters in the right order and making
them stay in the right place could be accomplished. But when
he was done, stretched across the page was a panting eel.

*

He blindfolded himself, bit his tongue, and slowly unspooled
his unknowable name. Waited thirty seconds. Took off his
blindfold. And behold—a line of delicate turtle dung.

*

Enough with trying to break the spell. He'd no longer
attempt to write his name. Instead, he would draw a circle.
And in the center of the circle, he'd add a blunt black navel.
But when he closed the circle and added the navel, he found
an onion. Dribbling a bit of soil.

EMERGENCY LOCATION SPELL

Yet there is anecdotal evidence that nonhuman sounds

cause the brain to identify faces in a crowded cup of snails.
My mother liked to pose with a penguin after she stunned

it with a rubber hammer. I can't stop wondering who

painted oceanic cows with blowholes on my bathrobe.
Your tongue goes milky white, pinkish purple, reddish

orange each time someone says: *But you did pay me to say*

every ten minutes: It's now 11:11. Alpha Centauri continues

to inquire: *Why am I not a deity unto you? And why does pasta
yearn so for dusk?* Salt, vaseline, wax, memory, honeyed lead.

While I was polishing the ambulance, you wrote all over

a bird: *Learn an infinite language.* You did pay me to open
a can of tuna fish so a myopic robot in the closet could watch

you watch. I'm getting infinite again, projecting myself

swooping through those worm holes in the back of the violin.
But you did pay me to say: *Emergency Location K can be found,*

as Basho wrote, just off the narrow path the junkyard moon follows

to the lower pond. It was and is and will be 11:11. So many
piano tuners does it take to calibrate the heart.

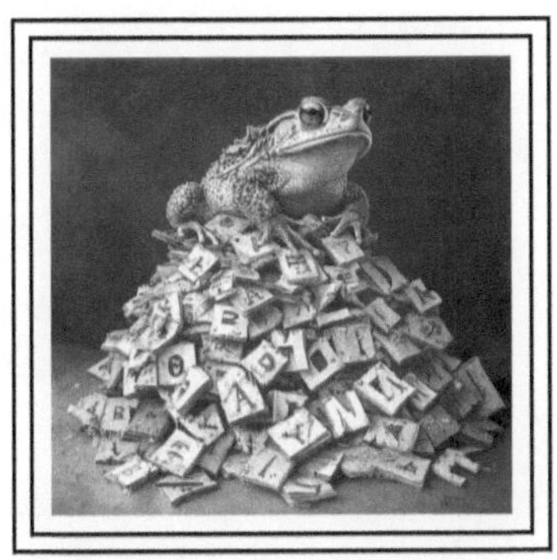

BOOK THREE

Five Definitions of *Spell*

Behold, a terrible thing said a beautiful thing to a rain
machine, hollow on the inside, camouflaged with baby
teeth on the outside.

*

Stuffing the mannequin with policed poetry, you knocked
over the jar of honey found in a tuba once owned by
Amelia Earhart.

*

*A red kimono. That's the blockage we found in your left
ventricle*, said the tree surgeon who had once taken a vow
of silence for ten years in Patagonia.

*

Despite wearing busy shoes made from newsprint,
a sickly child listens to a paintbrush smeared with Pepto
Bismol, to each ecstatic bristle.

*

*Yet you find you're at home in a cereal box, disassembled
clock, oval window, babbling gravel*, states the stately rupture
in the sky.

Never Sometimes Spell

Let us begin with a knot of wood, infinite loop, singing
bowl. As if I *never sometimes* dissolves into yellow-orange
chaos. Nonetheless, my lips again and again give way

to breath. Then I crawled into the Russian doll
with sea-glass skin. I jumped into the oil painting
of Spartacus and woke up reading your hair. *Everyone*

is your mother, says the *Book of Molecular Genesis*. It's hard
to believe a red verb palpitating on your shoulder. Imagine:
a small incision in the vertical churning light. Let us begin

with the five laws of the human skeleton. Suspend
the cabbage over the toad's broken alphabet. But wasn't
that you in the labyrinth using surveillance vernacular?

Given the choice between Lucien Freud's frozen leg
and a print shop in Seattle. Dirt teaches us how our bodies
pass through thousands of bodies. Only to begin.

Imagine: A star-starved sky, bread that tastes of sleep's
velocity, blanket with a small night bell sewn into each
corner, a many-legged desert that says: *Go on, go on.*

SPELL FOR A MARROW SPOON

I watched unstable holes fall through the sky over a comatose

cornfield. I watched inertia spread raspberry butter through
my chest, while my heart pondered granite dust forming

an inedible bible instructing nervous mannequins how to

conjure the infinite with a steel pole found in Amarillo.
Yes, I watched row on row of knives take wing over

a tobacco shop, desire dividing into millions of small red

clay squares. I watched you hug a buried stream
and state: *Distort the face with bark burnt and bottled in 1948.*

I watched your eyebrow float off as a bioluminescent butterfly

each day for fifty years. Someone's elbow saying: *We remind
you not to talk, even when swallowing.* But I was watching a hole

in the shape of a falling body form the next thing I would say.

As Blood Is the Fruit of the Heart Spell

As she was removing the shoplifting device from the white
        shirt
As was required of her by the motion and mechanics
        of her job
As the machine used to remove the device caught her finger
As she knew her finger would bleed even before it bled
As she didn't want blood upon the front of the new white
        shirt
As she was holding a Band-Aid in her other hand to keep
        it ready
As a long line of customers armed with clothing formed
        behind me
As she paged Jason or Jennifer to come to the front desk
        now please
As there can be no job without a Job no Job without a job
As I didn't want to call attention to her act of inattention
As I didn't want to insult the blood on the front of the white
        shirt
As blood adores compliments but is easily bruised
As it was her blood and not the store's or her supervisor's
As she explained how some shoppers remove shoplifting
        devices
As desire lurks in the blood no matter your zip code
As I listened while she complained which made me complicit
As I was a fellow bearer and lifetime spiller of that same fluid
As I could always take the shirt back when it wasn't her shift
As I didn't want her to be penalized for the action of her blood
As no one should have to apologize for the suction of a job
As ketchup or wine or olive oil would one day claim the shirt

As I left the store with the damp blotch on the shirt's
        whiteness
As the shoplifting scanner by the front door did not detect
        fresh blood
As blood contains beauty in movement but not beauty in
        stillness
As I gently washed the shirt relentlessly with cold water and
        soap once home
As blood calls for kindness even as it calls for erasure
As I couldn't bear to wear a bloodstained shirt to the wedding
As I knew my wife would see the blotch even before she saw
        the shirt
As I removed from the shirt the worker and the worker's
        error
As there is a drop of blood in our every article of clothing
As there can be no sorrow no ecstasy without a thread
        of blood
As blood is the fruit of the heart.

Spell for Living with the Dead

Protect yourself from anyone who collects teeth
in a leather cup.
Protect yourself from unfinished sleep
shed from a wakeful tree.
Each night the dead wash their hands
with salt and vinegar.

Make a soap with your first and last
listing utterance.
Make a soup with the crumbs of a crow's
crowded alphabet.
Behind your left eye, a small spark
that cannot be extinguished.

Protect yourself from anyone
who curls up inside a suitcase.
Protect yourself from anyone
who curls up inside an infinitive.
Behind your right eye, a disinterred elegy
for the disembodied.

This the century of silence:
ground, sifted, burned.
This the century of a palm tree
growing from a wound in the palm.
Each night lie back on that sea-glass
sofa that drifts across the desert.

Protect yourself from the sky
when it yawns mathematical blue.
Protect yourself from any spell
that breathes a bottomless breath.
Each morning wash your dead hands
with gasoline and sugar.

Spell for a Portrait with a Speck of Blood

Divide a drop of rain into dirt and divine, mumble
and motion. Certain words can turn the speaker

into a one-eyed god in a wind tunnel. An apple

bit a scalpel; an owl tolled your tongue. Is that
a piece of the moon on the sidewalk or a bite of a parched

pickle—chewed, limp, stiff. In my memory

of Hubert Humphrey, he's hollow, his face a smiley
Hubert Humphrey mask. Gamblers call it a tell,

the raised eyebrow, the slightest eyelid

twitch giving it all away. That blood speck
on your forehead—it could be claret, or ketchup,

or perhaps pasta sauce. Or is it the blood of a windowed

bluebird? Wine-red red is always wine-red red, unless
it's wine-red blue. In my portrait of the ex-president,

his radioactive red tie has shriveled. His tinny

tongue gone stiff, limp, chewed. Certain words can
translate a concrete shard into a silk peignoir,

a blister into a blood moon. The apple bit

my lip; my eye kilned the owl. When X = anything
greater than or less than X. In my portrait of Frida

Kahlo, she pauses before the mirror, tilts her head

as she eyes her sly double, saying: *When you leave me,
exit quietly, darling, through the mouth.*

SPELL: *PORTRAIT OF EDITH SCHIELE*, EGON SCHIELE, OCTOBER 28, 1918

Consider whether it matters we know
Edith, at this dying moment, dies
of the Spanish flu the day after

this last sketch of her by her husband.

Consider the tender, tousled hair,
the centered, unending stare of this figure
on the verge of napping, waking, turning

her head, wading back into sleep.

Consider how he can draw only her
beauty, not purpling flesh. That she
is six months with child. That

Egon, twenty-eight, a few days later dives

into that same pool where his wife
dissolved. Consider that moment
when Edith knew her husband's fluid

hand drew her out of her body.

Further Investigations into
    the Fear Response Spell

When nervous, I recite the list of the ninety-nine shades
of blue.
I have often dreamed that someone shaved my head
while I was sleeping.
Desire: To hear the rain's fetal feet and not hear your heart
stumbling to a stop.

Yes, star matter thrashed about your amygdala
on the mission back to Mars.
This is when you begin to admit you cannot unlock the door
with the touch of a starfish.
Subside your tongue, said the slug stuck to the side
of the priest's pale face.

When the body was reconstructed, crickets could be heard
singing in the woodwork.
Be quiet when you're quiet, said the lady with a slug stuck
to her shaved head.
Desire: To see nine black granite bowls floating
above the river.

If I were a factory, I would move about at night
on small, well-oiled wheels.
Wasn't that you eating a tablespoon of ash? said the slug
stuck to my thigh.
Your patience has the taste of black licorice left
in the freezer too long.

When nervous, I listen to the ninety-nine shades
of blue contract and dissolve.
On your shaved head, someone tattooed an eel exiting
the eye of a crow.
Desire: The destroying angel, its wings tangled
in the power lines.

SPELL: PHOTOGRAPH ENTITLED
NAZI NURSE WITH GERMAN CHILDREN, CIRCA 1941

We shall not be, tomorrow, what we were,
or what we are.
—Ovid, *Metamorphoses*, tr. A. S. Kline

The six children, four seated in small white
chairs, two seated on the floor, wearing
nothing but their underwear, appear relaxed,
as if they're attending a special party,
one where only light is served.

The nurse, clutching a bare-bottomed baby,
leans her head against the skull of the crying
child to demonstrate how deeply she cares
for her test subjects. All, even the baby,
wear goggles to protect their eyes

from the Neolithic light that will scientifically
lighten hair and eyes for a more Aryan
appearance, notes the caption. How
any form of light could lighten the eye,
I do not know, but this is a Nazi nurse,

and these are German children, and this
is a chamber only the dreamless could
enter. What about those two screens,
one behind and one in front of the children?
Is this moment filmed, preserving the thrill

of this brilliant experiment for posterity?
Or perhaps the screens indicate that live
images of the children, as they absorb
the magical rays, are being transmitted,
so administrators can sit at their desks,

watch a TV monitor, and nod, marveling
as hair and iris become ever fairer,
ever more Aryan. Look, on the far right,
one child cups his hands near his ears,
as if to better hear a distant voice.

But what can I tell him, other than
The cylinders of history turn, churn
the soil ceaselessly, without reprieve.
No, he's opened his hand to tell me,
Read my palm and I'll read yours.

Things I Should Apologize For Spell

Speaking to a smudge that once belonged to Marcus
Aurelius. Nazi-actors, cinematic hair, bituminous tea,
transparent teeth. My birthplace, a wheelbarrow, my

birthplace, a pencil, it follows. Stray words slipping

from a vague mouth at the airport: *Stay afloat.* Cheap,
abundant cirrus clouds from Abilene, afraid of the samba.
The trout in each part of the machine, machine in each

part of the trout. The river before it was a river, coiling

inside a scientist's belly. Ornate chair, mushroom spores,
diary cleansed by rusting scissors. Landfill music and rat
music consuming one another in the snow. Suit made

with rippling seaweed—dilating, contracting—it follows.
In the background, war radio saying, *Iron finger found
on the moon.* Rhizomatic architecture, triangular heart,

synaptical potatoes. Lives inside a lion I can't recall—

Sigmund Freud, falconry, idle foam. The river before
it was a river roiling inside a patent attorney's belly.
It follows. War radio in the background saying,

Iron finger found on the moon.

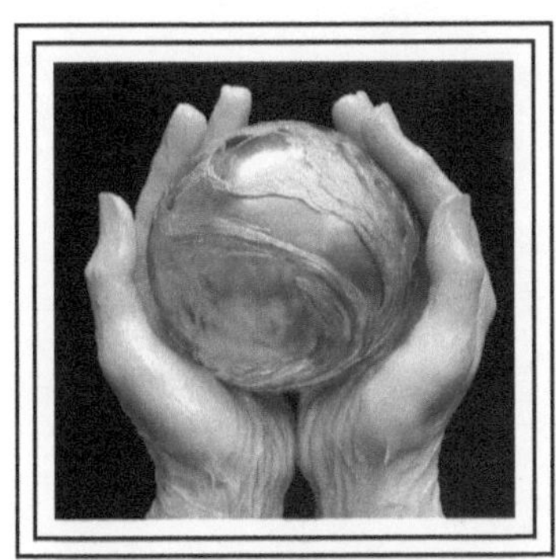

BOOK FOUR

Five Definitions of *Spell*

Protect yourself, said the barely heard barley
soup. *For any verb, cooked or uncooked, no
matter how friendly, may have rabies.*

*

It's only a small piece of glass from the star
factory in Bisbee, Arizona, stuck to your forehead,
sending out intermittent interstellar transmissions
of your wayward heartbeat.

*

Hummingbirds churn the incoherent light swelling
the curtains behind your eyes, which keep churning,
overflowing with incoherent light.

*

Five times a blue mercury orb melted my wax hands,
which keep hankering for the other side of the no-
nonce-none-natter-not.

*

Nibbling on impatiens, the equine-shaped cloud
carried lice that thrived for a spell on a gorilla
named Leopold who once composed a symphony
for a river of glass bells.

Monstrosity Spell

I eat only the long-ceased-moving, the suddenly-erased,
the shadow-no-longer-hinged-to-flesh.

This does not mean I am, to use your term, a monster.

I eat only the not-fully-visible, the self-disassembled,
Those with too-many-voices-flickering-in-the-spine.

A monster would never tell you this. A monster,

by definition, would try to seduce and devour. Often
at the same time. I won't eat a ceramic violin,

submerged cuckoo clock, fox-chewed red pinafore.

I don't eat your sleep or the organ you store it in.
A monster would say: *What I cannot eat glows, burns.*

And: *You cannot blame a monster for being a monster.*

See. I eat anyone who says: *This is my truth.* But only
because this is my truth.

SPELL FOR THE SECRET LIFE OF TEETH

Marianne Moore had
        engraved on each tooth:
I, too, dislike them.

Hubert Humphrey soaked his teeth
        each night
in a glass of akvavit.

Sophia Tolstoy loaned her teeth
        to a roving osteopath
and never saw them again.

Henry Kissinger hid his teeth
        along with that Nobel coin
in a bag of frozen peas.

Ava Gardner placed her teeth
        inside a cedar waxwing
in a velvet-lined cedar box.

Jack Spicer—remember? —
        called his teeth
love letters to Lorca.

Joan Didion, reading the mail,
        sharpened her teeth
with a triangular metal file.

Bishop Fulton Sheen bequeathed
        his teeth to a toothless monkey
in Kuala Lumpur.

Elizabeth Bishop pawned all her teeth
        for a taste
of tender armadillo brain.

THE MAN WHO COLLECTS PUTIN'S EXCRETA SPELL

I trust no one, not even myself.
–Joseph Stalin

He wears a bespoke silver suit
        with a zinc-gray tie to make you forget
                you once saw him washing his hands

with a small bottle of vodka in the baggage area
        at the airport. Last week, a reporter claimed
                she saw him at an oxygen bar in Moscow—

shoelaces loosened, head back, eyes glazed.
        It's said he doesn't like narrow hallways,
                the smell of rotting apricots, vowels

that elongate the mouth. It's said he's always
        followed by three aluminum
                hummingbirds. Before he sits down,

he scrubs the seat with an antiseptic
        wipe, looks to see who's watching, then
                scrubs the seat again. It's said his wife

wears a diamond made from the thigh bone
        of a bioengineer who tried to emigrate
                to Germany. It's said his teenage

daughter has cotton-candy-pink hair
        and had all her teeth replaced. If you
                happen to see him stroll by,

a black briefcase attached to the chain
          around his waist, three aluminum hummingbirds
                    trailing him, best not to smile or nod.

Best not to even think, *What does the great leader do*
          with all those packages of his waste?
                    Does he have them incinerated? Shipped off

to Siberia to be stored in a mine? Or does he
          stroll each night, barefoot, in his striped pajamas, to feed
                    his desiccated feces to the blushing roses.

Spell for Those Struck by a Conjunction
Traveling at the Speed of Ignorance

> *If you told me that I literally had to eat poop every*
> *single day and I would look younger, I might.*
> *I just might.*
> –Kim Kardashian

I'm pretty certain I would. No, I know I would
      eat poop at least once a day—if you told me
         all guns would decompose into rock salt

and burr. All the plastic in the ocean would turn
      into krill, kelp, coral song, tufted rain. I would gladly
         eat my poop. And yours. And yours.

If you told me Putin would become a baby
      tarantula under a rock on the sleepy soil of Siberia
         to be eaten by a larger tarantula. I would.

You would. We would eat Putin's poop right now
      with a side of polonium bacon. If you told me there
         would never be war of any kind, not with

missile, bomb, bullet, kiss. I would eat Kim Kardashian's
      literal poop. If you told me the planet grows younger,
         ever younger. O Lord, I'd eat your waste, too.

AND YOU SHALL KNOW US BY OUR TRASH:
AN ECO-POETICS SPELL FOR THE MOON

Ninety-six plastic bags of human waste
        (urine, feces, and vomit). *I sure feel bad,*
                said Buzz Aldrin, *for whoever finds my bag.*

More than seventy spacecraft,
        including modules and crashed orbiters.
                Twelve pairs of space boots.

Six nylon American flags (complete
        with artificial wind ripples)
                now bleached solar white.

Six gnomons. Five electric generators,
        each containing eight pounds
                of plutonium. Three lunar rovers,

one with a small Bible
        (James Irwin's) on the dashboard.
                Two golf balls (struck by Alan Shephard

with a six iron. *Miles and miles and miles,*
        said Shepherd on the flight of the second ball),
                location unknown. One bar of soap.

A falcon's feather (from Baggin,
        the Air Force mascot falcon) and a hammer
                (dropped simultaneously to demonstrate

Galileo's theory of falling objects).
        A color photo of James Irwin
                and another of Charles Duke, his wife,

and two kids—all bleached solar white.
        A polycarbonate urn containing human
                ashes (geologist Eugene Shoemaker).

Empty packages of space food.
        Insulating blankets. Several (improvised)
                javelins. TV cameras, film magazines,

tripod, zoom lens. Shovel, trenching tools,
        rakes, tongs, drills, brushes. Towels
                (red and blue), wet wipes, tissue dispenser,

anti-bacterial ointment, a pair
        of nail clippers. Earplugs, watchband,
                tie tack. Several hammocks.

One document proclaiming: *University
        of Michigan Alumni of the Moon*. One hundred
                $2 bills (forgotten by James Irwin

and Dave Scott, who planned
        to auction them—*Lunar-Infused $2 Bills!*—
                once back on Earth

to make a small fortune).
        I sure feel bad, said Buzz Aldrin, kicking
                from the door of the lunar lander

those *collection devices* full of human
feces, urine, and vomit onto the moon,
for whoever finds my bag.

Spell with Five Grains of Quietus

I can hear the slice of watermelon left on the cutting
board dazzle your succulent throat. In the street,
a turtle's sigh breaks the ocean into long prepositional
phrases. Snippets of brown hair left on the slate
floor say: *Soothe the heart with five grains of quietus,*

two of turbulence. Someone left the sticky honey
jar on the piano. The wife of the conductor, chewing
on a piece of sugarless gum, tells her lover, *Look,*
a fleshless messenger just slipped into that birch tree.
Soon to vanish into the inflamed eye of an angry god.

In the garden, an eyelash floats off in an aimless
breeze. Each guest wants hibiscus tea with a touch
of brandy. Leaves cling to the hair of the sleeping
babies. The former opera singer tells them: *Rub*
honey on the birch tree, my dear ones, when you wound it.

How to Live Forever

In memory of Spalding Gray

I heard you once give away this worldly wisdom: Never
turn off the radio on a word like *arson, cellulite, cancerous*

gingivitis, flood, suicide. That could only court bad luck.

I laughed at your cowardice. How could anyone ever
live like that? Then, weeks later, turning off the car

radio, I notice my hand hovering, waiting for just

the right word: *uptick, rescue, Vivaldi, cure, wingspan,
Elysian Fields, gum-o-flage.* Or would you say closing

on gum-used-to-disguise-the-hunter's-breath

constitutes lousy luck? Is that what caused
the head-on car collision on a back road in Ireland?

Which led to: *Body of Actor Found in East River?*

Spalding, look at what you've done. My hand, frozen
over the radio knob: *Red Sox down three to zip.*

An elephant places one palm-tree-size leg on top
of a landmine near a piece of newspaper smelling
of rotting fish. I watch *Lawless Order* to drown out
the throbbing car radios. The young man in camouflage
who attends to the elephant rides a scooter with a tiny tv
so he can see who's winning the war. I watch *Homicidal*

Order so there's one less homicide in the world. Camouflage
Pants slips a plastic garbage bag over the elephant's worldly
foot, what a mobile doctor does for a landlocked patient.
The chain around the elephant's neck protects the elephant
from wandering off and stepping on someone else's buried
anger. I watch *Victoria's Secret Order* so I'll know at what point

gender blurs into feather. If a mountain steps on a landmine,
will it give birth to another crater on the moon? Hold your
finger on a turnip, and you can feel the heartbeat of a flying
turtle. I watch *ER Order* because of what the police did
with a broom handle to a guy they called law-and-orderless.
The town installed a series of sleeping policemen across

a road to slow the traffic, though some insist you can't feel
the world's bumps while going 65 mph. I watch *Aryan Nation
Order* to see what fetishes will be appearing in the cornfield.
Some found the Virgin Mary sculpted from elephant dung
offensive, while others say during the attack she guided them
out of the movie theater. If you touch a neighbor's doorbell,

you could soon be bleeding parts of speech. A sleeper can
whirl a funnel cloud of sparrows, but can a sparrow wheel
a sleeper through a tunnel? After dinner, the table took
wing and next morning was found in the woods. Hold
your finger to a knife blade long enough and you smell fire.
I watch *Blooper Order* so I won't feel bad for the elephant

watching a tiny tv to see who's winning the war.

SPELL TO REPEL THE FUTURE

Build the brain with spanner wrench and boar rapture.
With crow ash and quartz and spider sonnet.
Build the brain with collapsible chair and baby powder.

With truffle and turnstile and fear of a flying fox.
Build the brain with binoculars and desert raincoat.
With oatmeal and walnut shell and blindfold.

Build the brain with shredded paper and shredded wheat.
With hammer and hummus and humming hailstone.
Build the brain with square wheel and milking stool.

With powdered milk and vellum and conjunction.
Build the brain with thumb tack and feathered cough.
With anaphora and piecrust and grappling iron.

Build the brain with titanium teeth and coffee bean.
With cinnamon and detective lung and global hair.
Build the brain with grocery list and goat grammar.

Build the brain with sunflower seed and unspooled rain.
With turtle shell amnesia and anonymous insomnia goggles.
Build the brain with the heart of owl or muskrat or whale.

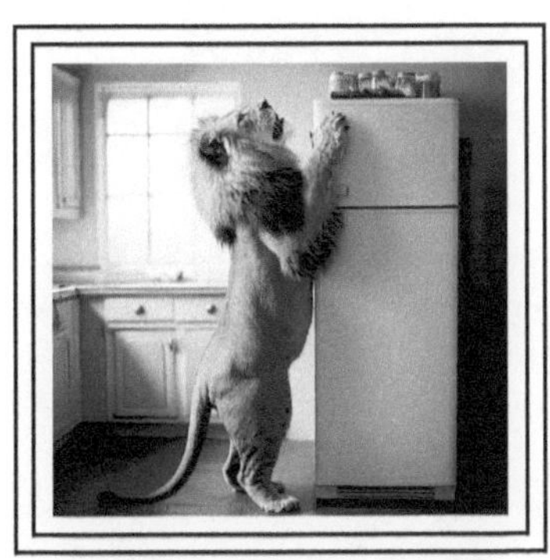

BOOK FIVE

Five Definitions of *Spell*

I touch crow brain cells, Civil War train station,
chewing gum on a casket, a sodden green voice
saying: *Let me spell you.*

*

*Over and over again, blood adores a functioning
waterwheel,* said the DNA taken from Napoleon's
soup spoon that was once encountered a potato
named Spume.

*

Before the bombs ever fell, the shock entered
through my fingers, overriding the early warning
detection system, and then the hand's autopilot
controls.

*

*I think Robert E. Lee is writing you once again,
with his need for another oxygen tank,* said the winter
light, pouring into the window of every train station
in your spine.

*

It wasn't the first time that I found a spell
of sparrows swirling in and out of the CAT scan
of my brain.

(Only a Fool Would Ever Make a)
Spell for a Drifting Bullet

The wind flips over
a torn scrap of paper

   and the bullet travels on

without pausing to consider
whether it will shatter

   wood or metal,

concrete, flesh, or glass.
The wind lifts into the air

   a shimmer

of hair then drops
the dead wisp back

   to the ground.

It doesn't really matter,
thinks the bullet. *Only my given*

   motion matters.

That's as far as a bullet
can go, speeding

   to its waiting home.

Spell for Lion, Colt, Cup of Blood

There's a lion in the house wearing my father's pajamas and silver-blue bathrobe. He makes snide comments, like *Three pianos were stabbed today in their grammar.* And *Adam, wearing a black leather harness and sporting rouged nipples, courted Eve, who kept a peripatetic serpent in her hair.* I will have to shoot this lion soon.

Where did my father leave his Colt .45? I look through the kitchen drawers and cabinets. There, next to the flour sifter, I find the gun and place it on top of the refrigerator, so the lion won't see it, but it will be easy for me to grab when needed.

No, I better keep the gun nearer. I slide it behind my back, my belt holding it in place. *What's with that lump growing out of your back, son?* says the lion, staring at me with concern. *You need to see a doctor pronto*, the lion advises. I notice the gun has shifted. It's now in front, pressing against my stomach.

Listen, son, says the lion. *I've been lodged inside your cheekbone for decades waiting to tell you this. One day, after a long silence, you'll say to the waiter,* Another cup of blood, please. *And the waiter will pull back the curtain covering one wall, and the surgical students in the classroom behind the glass wall will all stand and applaud.*

I pull out my father's gun and fire. A young girl I never noticed reaches out and catches the bullet. She holds it out to me in her hand and then swallows the bullet— without a glass of water. I shoot the lion in the leg. In each thick, bulky leg. He nods, as if he knew some vital part of my brain is missing. As if he, no, as if I were stuffed with glittering sawdust.

How to Tell Someone They're Slightly Fascistic

Don't say, *I'm afraid.* Don't say, *Wanda looks healthy,*
but there is nothing we can do. Don't say, *I'm moving*
to Sweden. Finland. Switzerland. Say, *Kristen and I*

are obsessed with Brussels sprouts. Say, *Don't you like*
Lala, the lingerie model? Say, *Sugar is sometimes just*
what you need when the weather turns ethereal.

Don't you feel better already? Weirder still, you need
not tell them fascism is inoperable and incurable.
Know that half-seduced and half-flummoxed is very

American. Don't say, *Kristen and I are very afraid*
of most terrestrial synergy. Conserve your erratic energy.
Don't say, *It seems we're never far from a dumpster.*

Say, *Isn't that a sexy underwater restaurant?* Slowly
almost state, almost don't, *Sometimes you need a trained*
psychiatrist to forget you need a trained psychiatrist.

ALL THE BEAUTY SPELL

In memory of Victoria Amelina (1986-2023),
Ukrainian writer and documenter of Russian
war crimes

A real beauty. That's how Russian Colonel General
Andrey Kartapolov describes the missile that uncoils
in a restaurant in Kramatorsk. Filled with civilians.

This is real beauty: A steel beam piercing warm
flesh. Unspun blood. A limb tossed to the roof
of a nearby car. This is *not a blow, but a song,*

rhapsodizes the colonel general, so overcome
by all the dread beauty that he never notices
he is the one who is dead. He, Andrey Kartapolov,

dead in heart, tongue, brain. Dead in bowel
and wrist, ankle and anus. Dead in knuckle,
wart, vein. Dead in each thick nostril hair.

Each thick, vomitous word. Even as he swoons,
woozy from all the sumptuous beauty
bestowed on him by the blown up and the burnt.

War Burrows Deep Spell

*It is good that war is so horrible, or we might grow
to like it.*
–Robert E. Lee

An angel with roots dangling
       from the bottom of its feet never
enters a trench. It perches askew
       on a severed tree or naps
inside an illustrated history
       of papier-mâché parrots.
In the trench, liquid music tremors
       the brain. A broken cup cannot hold
much song, but the sky presses
       each puddle to the ground.
An angel with aluminum eyes
       never appears near a soiled bandage
or a tongue coated with metallic ash.
       In an underground room off the trench
a large rat gnaws on the word *because*.
       An angel with rubber fingers
flickers inside a charred Toyota
       sinking into the mud beside a listing piano.
A flattened saxophone cannot
       hold much song, but pieces of the sky
press hard against each glass shard.
       An angel with nails for teeth
will tell you only this: *Let me kiss you
       on the neck, the knee, and here*
behind the ear. Above the trench
       the moon shatters into pinpricks

that glow, sizzle, dissolve.
       An angel with copper-wire hair
can be heard, swaying over the trench:
       Come, come see Joan of Arc, her
crown aflame, her crown of many flames.

Bomb-Shelter Futurism Spell

In a damp basement in Avdiivka,
a six-year-old girl named Varvara
draws a green alien with a black

eye that can see into the infinitely

finite future. It sees Vladimir Putin,
feet up on his fifty-five ton desk, staring
at a photo of Joseph Stalin. The sharp steel

bristles of Stalin's mustache could draw

blood from delicate tissue. Putin nods,
raises his vodka glass to Comrade Stalin
and says: *Great Leader, tell me,*

will I ever be as greatly feared as you?

The alien briefly shudders. Then
its blank eye sees a long, birch-bark-
like strip cradled in the soft hands

of a surgeon who has just sliced

and pried this listless metal tongue
from the back of a woman, whose flesh
will never let her forget. The alien tilts

slightly to one side, then quickly rights

itself. Now its blank eye sees a girl
in a dank basement. She's drawn
a green alien with one eye in the center

of its head. A reporter asks her:

Tell me, what can it see?
Can it see the end of this war?
No, says Varvara. *No one can see that.*

Spell for the Just and Unjust

The President finds a book, *Just and Unjust Wars*, on his Oval
Office desk. Without thinking, the President's hand reaches
out to the book, lining its edges perfectly with the corner of his
desk.

War is a people thing, he says to the book, *like a house made of
zucchini, or a zucchini made from a dead horse.*

*But with war, why haven't wild lions been brought before the court
for crimes against human flesh? And why haven't judges yelled,*
Bring me the fields of poppies who are killing our people with
their opioids? *Why?*

The President's forefinger taps the book several times, then
listens to hear if anyone inside taps back.

*After a battle, a soldier once told me he woke in a room filled with
mushrooms. Some mushrooms, they have many rooms, he told me,
so many rooms no one who has entered has ever returned.*

The President strokes the spine of the book, worrying a slight
crease.

I could have been a great general, but I fall asleep at the sight of blood.

Spell: Photograph of a Woman Embracing a Child's Body Wrapped in a White Shroud

If only we knew the child's name, height, weight, the color
      of their eyes and hair.

If only we knew the child's mother and father, had shared
      a meal, chatted over tea.

If only we knew if they were connected in any way to those
      who committed terror.

If only we knew who had slain the child, who had fired
      the missile, dropped the bomb.

If only we knew the exact place and time, could have watched
      it live as it occurred.

If only we knew the pilot who was involved, knew their heart,
      their hands, their family.

If only we knew the immediate reason, strategic purpose,
      the lasting consequences.

If only we knew where the child's body will be buried, who
      will be at the burial.

If only we knew who will visit the grave, what they will say
      over it.

If only we knew the right words to say, how to say them,
      and to whom.

If only we knew who will use this photograph, how it will be
        used, and why.

If only we could forget ever having seen this photo, know it
        exists, will always exist.

If only we could say we had nothing to do with it, nothing
        to do with any of it.

If only we knew the immediate reason, strategic purpose,
        the lasting consequences.

If only we didn't know the name of the five-year-old girl,
        the name of her aunt.

If only we could keep saying, *If only.*

Spell for Unspellable Peace

When the house shrunk, I was at the dinner
with a representative of the war, those spent eyes
shooting side to side. When the house expanded

the sky slipped through the basketball hoop,
floating in and out of the mouth of the mannequin
in the living room. The fire at end of the hall

pulling off its clothes. Wearing only a parachute
and kerosene-soaked shoes. *Carry your dead
to the dining room table. Talk with knife and fork*

and linen napkin, says the foul-mouthed smoke.
*The war eats the discarded, the bitter, the charred,
the broken down, the charmed, gazing up.*

*

Come back to me, Eurydice. Unfasten
my face. All trace of my hands, erase. Look
at that glassy spot where the moon appeared

to disappear. Walk us back into our bodies
inch by inch. Past the shot-through-the-head
words. Distant tools, out of control, flying

across the sky. Call to the moon at the bottom
of the swimming pool. Or is it a black shawl
shorn from the torn shadow on the wall.

Eurydice, you will find the war dead
in your rib, loin, inside right hip. All our dead
waiting for the motion of your lips.

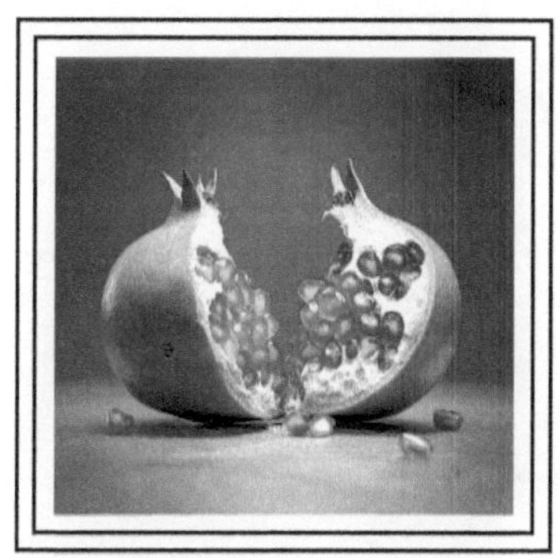

BOOK SIX

Five Definitions of *Spell*

If only you could completely let go of 3 a.m.,
the ragged heard, the barely said, the small
explosions in the weathered owl-smoke
quadrant.

*

*Words are dreadfully powerful, and words
uttered are ten times more powerful. The spoken
word is the science on which the entire universe
is built,* said the kindly exterminator, spraying
the base of the courthouse with pesticide.

*

After the many bouts of vertigo, sprinkled
throughout the ethics textbook you found
in a dumpster: Soothing-loose-ash-sunflower-
syllable-flight.

*

*You shall wear a loud crown in the physical
stratosphere,* said the baby's face spread across
the dawn lawn, *your tongue ever obedient
to the aphrodisiacal sun.*

*

Each undulating body flying through your
body, through rapturous rain of electricity,
the unbound tentacles swaying, saying:
Earth, be so alive.

Stopping by Words Spell

Whose words these are I think I know.
Who can really own them, though.
No one will see me stealing here
To watch these words become my own.

My sturdy tongue must think it weird
To mouth such blather far and near
Between your ears, that lovely space
Where song makes clatter something dear.

You give each word a goodly shake
And ask if this is some mistake.
This tune, so familiar, must leak
From the pillow used by Willy Blake.

These words are lovely, dark and deep,
But I have syllables to keep,
And text to eat before I sleep,
And text to eat before I sleep.

SPELL FOR THE BLACK ANGEL: AT THE OAKLAND CEMETERY, IOWA CITY, IOWA

You call yourself Rodina, but I know your name:
It's *Before You Worried Away Each Thumb to Nub.* It's
*When Misshapen Memory Is a Wing Rinsed in the Blackened
Earth.* It's *The Black Angel Carries the Sky on Her Back.*

I can offer you: a penny: a pen: my sweaty perambulations.
You look down: away: back to where one day you'll
lead us: to the iron cradle filled with oranges: still
warm from the forge. What was it my father

wanted to tell me: each time in the motel room
when his soft voice: broke: all I could hear was
the rustle of your wings: newspaper singeing
your fingers. I wanted to shake you: shudder

you back into silence: the iron ore before gesture.
You say I fallow the words wrong. I don't know who
I'm saying: what I speak with. One day I'll pause
before a stranger without thumbs: and then whoever

I've stung: however wrong: will I come undone.

SPELL: *JAMES DEAN POSES IN A CASKET*, FAIRMOUNT,
INDIANA, FEBRUARY 1955, DENNIS STOCK

Here you are, Jim, arms crossed over your not-yet-stilted
heart. At the intersection of prank and premonition, gag
and prologue, casket and latent catastrophe. Intersecting

mummery and mummy. *Just trying to get some rest, man,*

your lips almost mumble. Eyes closed, face at rest. Not all
that far from the grave of Cal Dean, your great-grandfather,
where you posed with your cousin Markie. Your unreal

hand on his all-too-real shoulder. Comforting the kid

with coffin-lining-soft comfort. Not yet at the intersection
of bravado and Brando. Porsche 550 Spyder and Ford Tudor.
Cellular anonymity and celluloid luminosity. *I don't have to*

explain anything to anybody, you said. But you did: *Take it easy*

driving. The life you save may be mine. At the intersection
of Route 466 and Route 41. Arterial speed intersecting
a man named Turnupseed. *Live fast, die young* colliding

with *Leave a good-looking corpse.* At the intersection of *head-on*

and *instantaneous. Crash* and *crush.* Eyes closed, motionless,
deathless, you wait—here, in your coffin, Jim. For the lid
to be shut tight. In seven months. Arms crossed over your

all-too-still heart. To embody velocity and never brake again.

While Waiting for the End of the World Spell

Right now a satellite observes man or a woman or a bundle

of rags in a ditch. Thomas Merton placed his ear to a maple
tree, held his breath, and listed. I asked for a bowl of green

pea soup at the airport food court and was told it would cost

four hundred and thirty-three crickets. A smartass told Sister
St. Molotov Cocktail that she had mispronounced the word

buoy, and the classroom hushed, as we prayed she wouldn't

ignite us. *Do not feel overly sad for the sharks electrocuted for their
serial crimes*, said the child tyrant. At the party, I asked

the Famous Poet if she really was the Famous Poet

and she said, *No, I'm John Lennon.* The voices of ants
burned through the steel door to the furnace room.

The only way out of your body, she told me, *is through the third*

rib, her finger pressing hard. Even now I cannot melt
a plastic soldier in the oven. This is what happens when

you find a snail shell in your shoe and you hear a bird

flying from the 1920s through your arm. Venetian
red doesn't quite taste like bittersweet immortality.

You can hear the future metastasize in John Brown's

batty cave. Once in Colorado I found myself gazing
at dozens of rattlers sunning themselves on a rocky shelf,

their lazy eyes calmly perforating me. Even when I say this

thirty-three times a day. The map of these United States
looks more and more like a boiled baby with a deadly rash.

SPELL FOR THE VORTEX NAPPING IN THE ATTIC

So I ran to Kazakhstan with a loose octopus that crawled
into someone's cornea and said, *Talk to me as if something*

you want is trying to kill you. Each summer, Lenin and Stalin

flirt with a medieval monk with live coals cocooning
in his long, undulating beard. As it so happens, I was

conjuring an ant swarm in an old mattress that once

crossed the Alps. When I look up, I see a man with delicate
ankles inside a coagulation of crows floating away. A friend

of mine, trapped in the bathroom for twenty-two years,

said, *I crave a mountain painted with birds, or else birds painted*
on a knife. Hovering around your face, a drowsy shark

from the Lewis and Clark expedition said: *I'm afraid your*

earhole still needs to breathe. As it so happens, I was taken
to a circular room to watch a lime trapezoid take flight

from the back of your skull. After I ate the bullet made

of clay, my back no longer ached. Each fall at the kitchen
table, I inhale the ashes of an elephant imprisoned for

making love to a hummingbird's reflection.

Anonymous baby tooth, wrapped in white thread, when spun
      pointing magnetic north.
Arthur Waley's *Translations from the Chinese*, translated by
      Son House, his hands dipped in hog blood.
Infertile doll constructed with twine, postage stamps, and
      termite wings.
The Mountain Poems of Stonehouse, translated by Jerry Lee Lewis's
      piano, eaten by Rachel Carson's cancer, transectioned
      by the dust between my toes.
One parsnip-eating turnip, as noted by the Society for the Care
      and Protection of Unknown Retrieval Systems.
Photo of night figure on rooftop chewing a stillborn mulberry
      infused with the Sea of Fecundity.
Poems of the Late T'ang mask, with tubes—inserted into eye, ear,
      and hair—delivering a constant clover-scented
      ether flow.
Recording of fire ants disassembling an armadillo corpse
      under a live oak in Andalusia, Alabama, circa 1883,
      titled *Should the Participles Boil Over*.
Sea urchin / plastic water bottle mask, not suitable for those
      with delicate leg or lung.
Shawl of woven armpit and milkweed hair, from
      the International Archive of Organic Arts, in Fedora,
      South Dakota, translated by Aldo Leopold.
Stork nest made from shredded Remedios Varo painting titled
      *Why It's Necessary to Keep Your Eyes Open Under Your
      Closed Eyelids*.
Stuffed mouse, in hardhat and denim overalls, sweeping mouse
      entrails (made of wood shavings).

Sunflower Splendor: Three Thousand Years of Chinese Poetry,
        translated by Merry Clayton, backed by the rain
        on Robert Johnson's snakeskin guitar.
Ten magenta raffle tickets for a near new pituitary gland.
Tethered otter tongue, known to babble: *Mrs. Charles Darwin*
        once asked the rushes and misshaped reeds to define eroticism.
        Exoticism? *they replied. That's easy. Just listen*
        to the hush of the rushes and reeds.
Turtle shell / burlap bag mask, some flaking about the lip.
The White Pony: An Anthology of Chinese Poetry, translated by
        Ali Farka Touré, scalded by the Yazoo River, impacted
        by a cup of star-ridden soil—breathing out, no,
        breathing through.

SPELL FOR A LATE DEPARTURE

(Repeat as needed)

I'll now remove my outer face
          and watch it float through
the space allotted you.

This is only to inform—
          not threaten pebble,
plant, or planet. No one

wants to loiter near
          an unstable table. If
you'll now allow me

to linger one moment
          more, I would then efface
my fungible form

from your visual array.
          Or to state it more
plainly: *I shall*

now peel away
          yet another layer
of my remaining remains.

Though in the process
          quite inadvertently
you, too, may dissolve.

We Need to Talk About the Pomegranate Spell

One quiet winter night, after I'm gone,
hold a pomegranate.

Plunge a knife,

slowly, tenderly, into the reddish flesh.
No one will cry out.

Break away

a white rib. Now gently loosen
a seed, surrendering it

to tongue and teeth.

That winter night, when I'm gone, remember
each seed swelling

with juice aches

to be broken. For it's true—the pomegranate
desires to be desired. Then

devoured.

There is nothing simpler, nothing
more complex. Look

at your red-stained hand.

WHEN YOU IMPRINT ONTO MY BACK
    THE MILKY WAY SPELL (IN 3-D, PLEASE)

Be sure, at each turn, the Milky Way may endure the zonal
flesh fluctuation. Be sure, if you can, of the unsayable,

the inextinguishable. The long-gone-to-unspun-rain must

surely be sure each element of syllable and linger saturates
Under the scrape of the moon and *Eat this and grow lightly mad.*

Moreover, be sure the embers cleanse what is called

the edible alphabet; cover it over with crack-in-the-skull
dust, which when inhaled brings the liver's lung ever further

into the goingness-unto-gone. Be sure, for you will be glad

of it, if the belly and the like do not steal the ever-more-
clear-brightness from the intestinal polar region

in the long turning. Be sure, moreover, the Milky Way,

in breathing iron and ocean, stammer and yaw, will translate
me far beyond the reach of unforeseen mummification,

even as another vehement heat will have found me.

As you ingest this, be sure joy is mingling about your middle,
for the agitated will run about the sky even as the sky grows

amongst us ever more agitated. And be sure, even unto

the unsure, my once-green lizard tongue speaks to those
bound to ankle, bowel, knuckle, hair. Moreover, be sure,

even now, I breathe in every place the Milky Way

does give breath, which will, I know, break me. Burst
me into silky, crumbling light. Into: *The dust glistens, listens*

to all that stirs. Into: *Let this, too, abide.* Into: *So do all*

living creatures, knowing and unknown, venture forth
wherever they roam, the Milky Way adrift on their back.

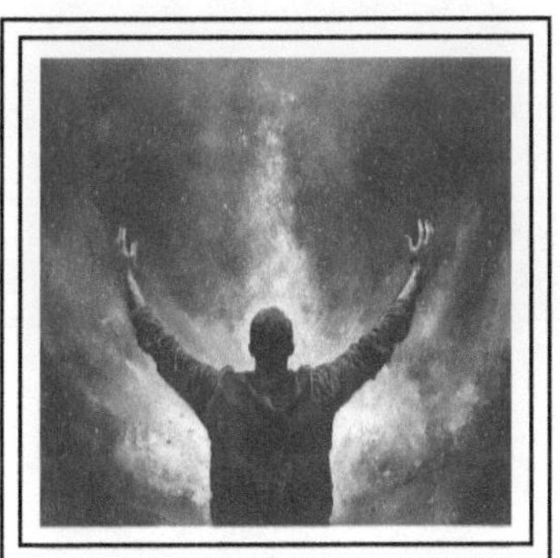

NOTES

"Placental Gravity Spell" was inspired by Gregory Pardlo's "Written by Himself."

"Spell for a Piece of Mt. Everest Glowing in a Suitcase" is in memory of Tomaž Šalamun.

"Because Everyone Loves a Love Spell, However, Whosoever" is in memory of Kent Johnson.

"Spell for the *Barbenheimer* Mutations": All the images in the poem describe online *Barbenheimer* memes.

"All the Beauty Spell": Thirteen civilians were killed and sixty wounded by this Russian missile fired on June 27, 2023.

"Spell: Photograph of a Woman Embracing a Child's Body Wrapped in a White Shroud": This photograph, taken by Mohammed Salem, shows Inas Abu Maamar holding the body of her five-year-old niece Saly.

"Five Definitions of *Spell*" (Book 6): *Words are dreadfully powerful, and words uttered are ten times more powerful. The spoken word is the science on which the entire universe is built* was stated by Sinead O'Connor.

"Spell for the Black Angel: At the Oakland Cemetery, Iowa City, Iowa," is for Joe Gastiger.

"Spell: *James Dean Poses in a Casket*, Fairmount, Indiana,
February 1955, Dennis Stock" : For a public safety ad,
Dean was supposed to say, *The life you save may be your own.*
Dean ad libbed: *The life you save may be mine.* The vehicle
Dean collided with was driven by Donald Turnupseed.

ABOUT THE AUTHOR

JOHN BRADLEY was born in Brooklyn, New York, and grew up in Framingham, Massachusetts; Lincoln and Omaha, Nebraska; Massapequa and Lynbrook, New York; and Wayzata, Minnesota. His first book, *Love-in-Idleness: The Poetry of Roberto Zingarello*, won the Washington Prize, in 1989, and a second edition, expanded and revised, was published by Word Works. Besides writing poetry, he is also fond of composing aphorisms, some of which appear in the anthologies *Short Flights* and *Short Circuits*. He's been a reviewer of poetry books for *Rain Taxi* for many years. The recipient of two National Endowment for the Arts Fellowships, a Pushcart Prize, and a grant from the Illinois Arts Council, he's currently a poetry editor for *Cider Press Review*. He lives in DeKalb, Illinois, with his wife, Jana, and their cats, Kiki and Zuzu.

Learn more at: johnbradleypoetry.com.

ACKNOWLEDGMENTS

Thanks to the editors of the following publications in which
some of these poems first appeared, sometimes in an earlier
version:

Anvil Tongue: "Spell for Those Struck by a Conjunction
           Travelling at the Speed of Ignorance"
Autumn Sky Poetry Daily: "Bomb-Shelter Futurism Spell"
The Bitter Oleander: "Spell for the Just and Unjust"
Caesura: "How to Live Forever"
Calibanonline: "When You Imprint onto My Back the Milky
           Way Spell (In 3-D, Please)"
Conflict, Tragedy, Resolution (website): "Spell: Photograph of a
           Woman Embracing a Child's Body Wrapped in a
           White Shroud"
Dispatches from the Poetry Wars: "And You Shall Know Us
           by Our Trash: An Eco-Poetics Spell for the Moon"
Heavy Feather Review: "Premonition That a Book Will Take
           the Shape of a Spellbound Bird" and "Spell for the
           Vortex Napping in the Attic"
International Times: "All the Beauty Spell," "The Man Who
           Collects Putin's Excreta Spell," and "Spell for the
           Barbenheimer Mutations"
The Kerf: "(Only a Fool Would Ever Make a) Spell for a
           Drifting Bullet," and "Stopping by Words Spell"
Map Points: "Packing for Earth 2.0 Spell"
The Non-Materialism Foundation: "Spider Spell(s)"
The North American Review: "Spell for a Marrow Spoon"
Otoliths: "(Further Evidence of a) Spontaneous Mummification
           Spell," and "Spell for the Secret Life of Teeth"
Pedestal: "Things I Should Apologize for Spell"

The Prose Poem: "Spell for Lion, Colt, Cup of Blood"
Red Dirt: "Spell for the Persistence of Desire"
SurVision: "Placental Gravity Spell," and "Spell for a Piece
      of Mt. Everest Glowing in a Suitcase"
Terra Incognita: "Spell for a Six-Sided Head"

Some of the poems also appeared in the following publications:

*And Blue Will Rise Over Yellow: An International Poetry
      Anthology for Ukraine*, Kallisto Gaia Press: "Bomb-
      Shelter Futurism Spell"
I Once Met Kent Johnson, Shuffaloff Press: "Because Everyone
      Loves a Love Spell, However, Whosoever"
The Night's Musician: Poems About the Moon, Negative Capability
      Press: "Twenty Questions for the Moon (Not That It
      Needs a Spell)"
*Poetics for the More-Than-Human World: An Anthology of Poetry
      and Commentary*, Dispatches Editions: "And You Shall
      Know Us by Our Trash: An Eco-Poetics Spell for the Moon"
The Poetry of Capital: Voices from Twenty-First Century America,
      Univ. of Wisconsin: "As Blood Is the Fruit of the Heart Spell"
Spontaneous Mummification, SurVision Books: "As Blood Is the
      Fruit of the Heart Spell," "Spell for the Black Angel,"
      "The Glue Between the States Spell," "Spell for the
      Just and Unjust," "Placental Gravity Spell," "When
      You Imprint onto My Back the Milky Way Spell
      (In 3-D, Please)"

OTHER BOOKS BY JOHN BRADLEY
PUBLISHED BY DOS MADRES PRESS

EVERYTHING IN MOTION, EVERYTHING AT REST:
A GALLERY OF PHOTO POEMS (2020)

HOTEL MONTPARNASSE - LETTERS TO CESAR VALEJO
(2021)

DEAR MORPHEUS, THE GLUE THAT IS YOU (2022)

FOR THE FULL DOS MADRES PRESS CATALOG:
www.dosmadres.com

www.ingramcontent.com/pod-product-compliance
Lightning Source LLC
Chambersburg PA
CBHW021326060726
47591CB00006B/1895